D0258811

A Constitution for Europe

Constitution adopted
by the Heads of State
and Government

Presentation
to citizens

Information document produced
by the Commission. It has no legal
status and does not necessarily reflect
the views of the European institutions.

 EUROPEAN UNION

Table of contents

1. Origin and development of the Constitution

Over the past 15 years, the history of the European Union has been marked by a series of changes to the European Treaties. Each one was prepared by an Intergovernmental Conference (IGC) bringing together, over a period of months, the representatives of the governments of the Member States. The Commission also took part in the work of the IGCs, and the European Parliament was also involved.

Treaties regularly revised

The **Single European Act**, signed in February 1986, enabled the Union to create the single market and establish on its territory freedom of movement for people, goods, services and capital, from which the business sector and the people of Europe now benefit.

The **Maastricht Treaty**, signed six years later, in February 1992, enabled the Union to move forward in a number of areas: the introduction of a single currency, a common foreign policy, cooperation in the area of justice and home affairs.

After Maastricht, however, the further development of the European political union seemed to lose its momentum. The two IGCs which led to the signing of the **Amsterdam (1997) and Nice (2001) Treaties**, even though moderately successful, were characterised by a weaker political resolve and many institutional questions, capitally important though they were on the eve of the Union's enlargement, remained unanswered (how to ensure the smooth running of a Union of 25 or more Member States, how to guarantee the legitimacy of the institutions representing the States and peoples of Europe).

Need for institutional reform to serve the enlarged Union

When, in December 2000, the Heads of State and Government of the 15 Member States, meeting in **Nice**, reached an agreement on the revision of the Treaties, they felt the need to pursue the institutional reform which many deemed too timidly expressed in the Treaty of Nice. The European Council accordingly instituted a **broader and more comprehensive debate on the future of the Union** with a view to fresh revision of the Treaties.

The stimulus provided by the Nice European Council

Laeken Declaration

A year after Nice, the European Council met in **Laeken** and, on 15 December 2001, adopted the Declaration on the Future of the European Union, committing the Union to becoming more democratic, more transparent and more effective, and paving the way for a Constitution in response to the expectations of the people of Europe.

The Convention: a new, more open and more transparent method of revising the Treaties

The **method** used so far to revise the Treaties has come in for much criticism. European integration is a matter for all our citizens. The major stages in its development can no longer be decided at Intergovernmental Conferences held behind closed doors and involving only the leaders of the governments of the Member States. In order to prepare the next IGC in as transparent and as wide-ranging a way as possible, the European Council therefore decided to convene a **Convention** bringing together the main stakeholders in the debate: representatives of the governments of the 15 Member States and the 13 candidate countries, representatives of their national parliaments, representatives of the European Parliament and of the European Commission, 13 observers from the Committee of the Regions and the European Economic and Social Committee, plus representatives of the European social partners and the European Ombudsman. The Convention method has made it possible for the first time for all European and national viewpoints to be expressed in a broad, open and transparent debate.

Mandate of the Convention: to provide a response to various questions on the future of Europe

The **mandate** of the 105 member of the Convention and their alternates, under the chairmanship of Mr Giscard d'Estaing, was established by the Laeken European Council. The aim was to examine the essential questions raised by the future development of the Union, and to seek out responses to be presented in a document which would be used as the starting point for the negotiations of the IGC, which, as set out in the Treaty on European Union, would take the final decisions. Certain issues had been identified by the Laeken European Council: how to ensure better distribution of the Union's powers, how to simplify the instruments whereby the Union takes action, how to provide better guarantees of democracy, transparency and effectiveness in the European Union, how to simplify the current Treaties, and whether this simplification could pave the way for the adoption of a European Constitution.

Organisation of the work of the Convention: a Chairman, Mr Giscard d'Estaing, a Praesidium to guide its work

In order to guide the debates of the Convention a **Praesidium** was set up, composed of 13 key figures: the Chairman, Mr Giscard d'Estaing and two Vice-Chairmen, Messrs Amato and Dehaene, representatives of the governments of the three Member States which held the Presidency of the Council during the Convention, two representatives of the national parliaments, two representatives of the European Parliament and two representatives of the Commission (Messrs Barnier and Vitorino). The representative of the Slovene Parliament was invited to take part in the meetings.

The first session of the Convention was held on **28 February 2002**. The Convention met over a period of 15 months in **plenary sessions** lasting two or three days and involving one or two meetings monthly in the premises of the European Parliament in Brussels. In parallel with the Convention's plenary sessions, work was also organised within **working groups** or think tanks, each chaired by a member of the Praesidium and focusing on a series of specific topics.

Plenary sessions and working groups

In the interests of transparency, a Convention **Internet site** (http://european-convention.eu.int) published the contributions of the members of the Convention, the proceedings of the debates and the draft texts debated.

An Internet site

In order to further widen the debate and involve all the people of Europe, a plenary session of the Convention was devoted to listening to civil society. Contact groups, along the lines of the working groups, also enabled the civil society organisations to put forward their points of view.
Civil society forum

Civil society forum

A forum was opened for these organisations (social partners, business circles, NGOs, academic world, etc.), which thus had the opportunity to post on a dedicated Internet site (http://europa.eu.int/futurum/forum_convention) their contributions to the debate on the future of the Union.

The Futurum site (http://europa.eu.int/futurum) has continued to publish all documents and links related to the debate on the future of the European Union.
Futurum

Futurum

After more than a year of debates, the Convention reached a consensus to forward a draft Constitution to the European Council.

Convention consensus to submit a draft Constitution in preparation for the Intergovernmental Conference

Presentation of the Convention's draft Constitution to the European Council

Mr Giscard d'Estaing accordingly presented the results of the work of the Convention to the **Thessaloniki European Council** on 20 June 2003.

In the view of the European Council, the draft constitutional Treaty prepared by the Convention marked a historic step forward in the efforts to complete European integration, i.e. by bringing the Union closer to its citizens; strengthening our Union's democratic character; and facilitating our Union's ability to act as a coherent and unified force on the world stage and effectively meet the challenges of globalisation. The European Council took the view that the Convention had proved its worth as a forum for democratic dialogue.

Following a final meeting of the members of the Convention, the final draft Constitution was submitted to the Presidency of the European Council in Rome on 18 July 2003.

The work of the Intergovernmental Conference

The text submitted by the Convention served as the basis for the work of the **Intergovernmental Conference**, which brought together the representatives of the governments of the 25 current Member States, the European Commission and the European Parliament. The three candidate countries – Bulgaria, Romania and Turkey – also took part in all the meetings of the IGC.

The IGC met several times from October 2003 onwards at Foreign Minister level and at Head of State and Government level. At the European Council in Brussels on 17 and 18 June 2004, the IGC brought its work to an end after eight months of negotiations, with agreement having been reached between the governments of the 25 Member States. The documents relating to the work of the IGC have been published on the Council's IGC website (http://ue.eu.int/cms3_fo/showPage.ASP?id=251&lang =fr).

Having been adopted by the Heads of State and Government, the Constitution will be signed by them and then ratified by each Member State in line with its own constitutional arrangements (i.e. by parliamentary procedure and/or by referendum). The Constitution will not take effect until it has been ratified by the 25 Member States.

2. What does the Constitution look like?

The Constitution puts forward a **single text** to replace all the existing Treaties in the interests of readability and clarity.

A single text: the European Constitution

It consists of four parts.

Four parts

Part I contains the provisions which define the Union, its **objectives**, its **powers**, its decision-making **procedures** and its **institutions**.

I. The Constitution's fundamental provisions

The **Charter of Fundamental Rights**, solemnly proclaimed at the Nice European Council in December 2000, has been incorporated into the European Constitution as Part II.

II. Charter of Fundamental Rights

Part III of the Constitution focuses on the Union's **policies** and actions, and incorporates many of the provisions of the current Treaties.

III. The Union's policies

Part IV contains the final clauses, including the **procedures for adopting** and **revising** this Constitution.

IV. The final clauses

3. A Constitution for the citizens of Europe

3.1 The Union's values and objectives

A Union of peoples and states

The European **Constitution** establishes the European Union, a **union of the peoples and States of Europe**. This Union is **open** to all **European countries** which respect its values and undertake to promote them jointly.

The Union's values

The Constitution sets out the values on which the Union is based: respect for **human dignity, freedom, democracy, equality**, the **rule of law**, and respect for **human rights**. These values are common to the Member States in a society characterised by **pluralism, non-discrimination, tolerance, justice, solidarity** and **equality between women and men**.

The Union's symbols: flag, anthem, motto, currency and Europe Day

Several of the Union's symbols have been enshrined in the Constitution. The European flag consists of a circle of 12 gold stars on a blue background. The European anthem comes from the Ode to Joy from Beethoven's ninth symphony. The Union's motto is "United in diversity". The currency of the Union is the euro and 9 May is celebrated as Europe Day throughout the European Union.

Fundamental freedoms and non-discrimination

Freedom of movement for people, goods, services and capital, and **freedom of establishment**, are guaranteed by the Union throughout its territory. The Constitution prohibits all **discrimination** on grounds of **nationality**.

The Union's objectives

The aim of the Union is to **promote peace, its values and the well-being of its peoples**. It offers its citizens an area of freedom, security and justice, and a single market in which competition is free and undistorted. It strives for a Europe of **sustainable development** based on balanced economic growth, price stability, a highly competitive social market economy, a high level of protection and improvement of the quality of the environment. It fosters **scientific and technical progress**. It takes action to stem **exclusion and discrimination**, and promotes **justice and social protection, gender equality, inter-generational solidarity** and protection of **children's rights**. The Union promotes economic, social and territorial **cohesion** and **solidarity** between its Member States.

Instruments to serve the Union's objectives

In order to attain these objectives, the Union has certain **powers** which are conferred upon it in the Constitution by the Member States. These powers are exercised using the **Community method** and specific instruments within a **single institutional framework**.

The Union must respect the equality of the Member States before the Constitution. It must also respect the **national identity** of its Member States, inclusive of regional and local self-government. Likewise, it must respect the **essential functions of the State**, including those for ensuring territorial integrity, maintaining law and order and safeguarding national security. By virtue of the **principle of loyal cooperation**, the Union and its Member States, in full mutual respect, will assist each other in performing the tasks stemming from the Constitution. The Member States help the Union to fulfil its mission. They must refrain from any measures which could jeopardise the attainment of the objectives set out in the Constitution.

The Union and the Member States

The Union has a legal personality to assert and uphold its values and interests in the international arena. It contributes to peace, security, the sustainable development of our planet, solidarity and mutual respect among peoples, free and fair trade, eradication of poverty and protection of human rights, especially children's rights, and respect for and consolidation of international law.

The Union and the rest of the world

The Constitution and the law adopted by the Union when exercising the powers assigned to it take precedence over the national law of the Member States.

Union law has primacy over the national law of the Member States

3.2 European citizenship and fundamental rights

3.2.1 European citizenship

Citizenship of the Union complements national citizenship and does not replace it.

Citizenship of the Union to complement national citizenship

The Constitution clearly asserts the rights which stem from citizenship of the Union: the right to **move and reside freely**, **the right to vote and to stand as candidates in elections to the European Parliament** and in **municipal elections**, the right to **diplomatic and consular protection**, the right to **petition the European Parliament** and the **right to refer matters to the Ombudsman** and **to write to the institutions in one of the Union's languages** and receive a reply in that same language.

List of rights which citizens of the Union enjoy

The above list is by no means exhaustive and other rights of citizens of the Union are listed in a specific section of the Constitution devoted to "The democratic life of the Union"; this refers to the opportunity to express and exchange views on all areas in which the Union takes action and the **right of access to documents** produced by the Union's institutions.

Part of the Constitution is devoted to democratic life

3.2.2 Fundamental rights

The Charter of Fundamental Rights is an integral part of the European Constitution

The text of the **Charter of Fundamental Rights** had been approved by a previous Convention. The Parliament, the Council and the Commission solemnly proclaimed the Charter on 8 December 2000. However, the Charter was not part of the Union's Treaties and had no binding legal force.

The Constitution thus achieves a major breakthrough which allows the Union to have its own **catalogue of rights**. The Charter is incorporated into the Constitution as Part II; its provisions have binding legal force but this does not mean an extension of the Union's powers.

The institutions, bodies and agencies of the Union must respect the rights written into the Charter. The same obligations are incumbent upon the Member States when they implement the Union's legislation. The Court of Justice will ensure that the Charter is adhered to.

The content of the Charter has undergone no changes in relation to the text drafted by the previous Convention, and only amendments of form have been made.

The content of the Charter is broader than that of the **European Convention for the Protection of Human Rights and Fundamental Freedoms (ECHR)** signed in Rome on 4 November 1950 and ratified by all the Member States of the Union. Indeed, whereas the ECHR is limited to civil and political rights, the Charter of Fundamental Rights covers other areas such as the right to good administration, the social rights of workers, the protection of personal data and bioethics.

Accession of the Union to the European Convention on Human Rights

Under the terms of the current Treaties, the Union had no competence to accede to the ECHR. By contrast, the Constitution makes explicit provision for the future accession of the Union to the ECHR. As for the incorporation of the Charter into the Constitution, accession to the ECHR does not mean any change to the Union's powers as defined in the Constitution. The full incorporation of the Charter and accession to the ECHR are complementary rather than alternative steps.

3.3 Who does what in the Union? Clarification of powers

One of the key contributions of the Constitution is that it clarifies the Union's powers or competences and the respective roles of its institutions.

Classification of powers

The Union can act only within the limits of the powers vested in it by the Constitution. The Constitution sets out clearly the matters for which the Member States have **conferred power to act on the Union** and indicates the **categories of Union competence**.

A first category is made up of certain very specific areas where the Union acts alone on behalf of all the Member States. These are **"exclusive" competences**. It has been considered that by definition an action at Union level is more effective than disjointed action by each of the Member States.

Exclusive Union competence

This category covers the following:
- customs union;
- establishment of competition rules necessary for the functioning of the internal market;
- monetary policy of Member States whose currency is the euro;
- conservation of marine biological resources under the common fisheries policy;
- common commercial policy.

A second category groups the areas in which the Union acts when its action brings added value to action taken by the Member States, sometimes in a very comprehensive way. These are called **"shared competences"**.

Shared competences

This category covers the following:
- internal market;
- certain aspects of social policy;
- economic, social and territorial cohesion;
- agriculture and fisheries, except conservation of marine biological resources;
- environment;
- consumer protection;
- transport;
- trans-European networks;
- energy;
- area of freedom, security and justice;
- certain aspects of common safety concerns in the field of public health;
- certain powers in the fields of research, technological development and space;
- certain powers in the fields of development cooperation and humanitarian aid.

Coordination of national economic and employment policies In certain other areas, namely economic and employment policies, the Member States recognise that their national policies need to be coordinated within the Union.

A common foreign and security policy The Constitution also stipulates that the Union has competence to define and implement a common foreign and security policy, including the progressive framing of a common defence policy.

Supporting competences In the final category of powers, of a **"supporting" nature**, the Union acts only to coordinate or supplement **action taken by the Member States**, which thus retain very substantial freedom of action and the primary responsibility for management in relation to their citizens. The Union cannot harmonise national legislation in these areas.

This category covers the following:
- measures to protect and improve human health;
- industry;
- culture;
- tourism;
- education, youth, sport and vocational training;
- civil protection;
- administrative cooperation.

A flexibility clause complements the classification of powers In order to retain some degree of **flexibility** in the system, there is a clause which allows the Council to plug any gaps in the powers conferred upon the Union whenever action at Union level is called for in order to attain one of the objectives of the Constitution. In such cases, the Council will take a unanimous decision after approval by the European Parliament.

3.4 The principle of subsidiarity: ensuring the proper exercise of powers

The principle of **subsidiarity** is designed to ensure that whenever the Union exercises its powers it acts only to the extent that such action is actually required and brings added value to action taken by the Member States. The principle of subsidiarity is designed to ensure that decisions are taken as closely as possible to the people, checking constantly that the action to be taken at the Community level is justified in relation to what is possible at the national, regional or local levels. The principle of **proportionality** targets the same objective of ensuring proper exercise of powers, stipulating that the content and form of action taken by the Union must not go further than what is necessary to attain the objectives of the Treaty.

The principles of subsidiarity and proportionality

The Constitution strengthens the application of both principles. When the **Commission** makes a proposal, it must **explain** the way in which it has taken these two principles into account. For the first time, every **national parliament** will be able to re-examine the proposals and issue a reasoned opinion if it considers that the principle of subsidiarity has not been respected. If one third of the parliaments hold the same opinion, the Commission will have to review its proposal.

A new mechanism to ensure compliance with the principle of subsidiarity...

A last level of control is triggered upon the adoption of a law: the right of referral to the **Court of Justice**.

...plus a jurisdictional control

3.5 A legitimate and democratic Union

The Constitution for the first time defines the **democratic bases** of the Union and gives them more tangible expression.

Democratic participation as a cornerstone of the Union

The Constitution imposes new obligations on the institutions with regard to **consultation** of **civil society**, **transparency**, access to documents and respect for personal data. In addition, the role of the **social partners** is anchored in the Constitution. The Union will also engage regularly in dialogue with churches and non-confessional organisations.

How to achieve better democratic participation?

The Constitution also introduces a new mechanism which allows direct input from Union citizens, if they number at least a million and represent a significant number of Member States. Using this new mechanism, citizens can ask the Commission to submit to the legislator a legislative proposal which they consider necessary.

Laws initiated by citizens

Holding the majority within the Convention, the members of the **national parliaments** prompted the members of the Convention to seek ways of enhancing the role of the national parliaments in European integration. The **transparency of the Council's work** will enable the parliaments to better monitor the positions of their governments within the Council, and the **"early warning" mechanism concerning respect of the principle of subsidiarity** will offer them a direct way of influencing the legislative process. Through this mechanism, the national parliaments will be informed about any new action taken by the Commission and, if a third of them consider that a proposal does not comply with the subsidiarity principle, the Commission will have to review its proposal. Better inter-parliamentary cooperation will also strengthen the role of the parliaments within the Union.

3.6 Union membership

Joining the Union:
obligation to respect
the values of the Union

In order to join the Union, a European State must **respect the value**s of the latter.

The accession of a State requires a **unanimous** Council decision, the approval of the European Parliament, and ratification of the accession agreement by all the Member States.

Suspension of rights
in the event of violation
of the Union's values

By a decision taken unanimously (not counting the State concerned) and after approval by the European Parliament (voting by two-thirds majority), the European Council can indicate **serious** and persistent **violation of the Union's values by a Member State**, after which the Council may, by qualified majority, suspend the rights of the Member State in question.

Introduction in the Constitution
of the option for a Member
State to withdraw from
the Union

Any Member State can decide – and this is an innovation introduced by the Constitution – in accordance with its constitutional rules, to **withdraw from the Union**. Its relations will, in this event, be governed by an agreement between itself and the Union.

4. The institutions and the European project

In order to carry forward the European project and enable the Union to attain its objectives, an effective and legitimate institutional framework is needed. This dual need is even more important in an enlarged Union of 25 or more Member States. The Constitution includes the bulk of the existing institutional provisions and introduces two new institutional elements: a more stable Presidency of the European Council and a Foreign Affairs Minister.

4.1 The Union's institutional framework

Under the terms of the Constitution, the institutional framework as such includes the **European Parliament**, the **European Council**, the **Council of Ministers**, the **European Commission** and the **Court of Justice of the European Union**.

The European Central Bank (ECB) plays a major role in the Union's economic and monetary policy, while the Court of Auditors ensures auditing of the Union's revenue and expenditure.

Alongside these institutions stand two advisory bodies, the **Committee of the Regions** and the **European Economic and Social Committee**.

4.1.1 The European Parliament

The European Parliament is the institution in which the people of the Member States are represented. In most areas, Parliament has a role of **co-legislator**, stands as the **budgetary authority** alongside the Council, and also exercises some **political control** over the Commission.

The European Parliament: legislative, budgetary and political control

The Constitution strengthens the European Parliament's powers as co-legislator by extending to new areas the scope of the so-called codecision procedure, henceforth termed **legislative procedure**, whereby Parliament takes joint decisions with the Council.

Extension of the jointly decided legislative procedure of Parliament and the Council

The number of Members of the European Parliament, elected by direct universal suffrage, for a five-year term, is established at a maximum of 750. In accordance with a principle of degressive proportionality, each Member State has a minimum of 6 and a maximum of 96 seats. The exact number of seats allocated to each Member State will be decided before the European elections in 2009.

A maximum of 750 Members of the European Parliament

4.1.2 The European Council

Role of the European Council

The European Council is the institution responsible for giving the Union the **political impetus** needed for its development. It does not exercise legislative functions. Generally speaking, it takes its stand by **consensus**. The Constitution provides for one European Council meeting every quarter.

Composition of the European Council

The European Council is composed of the **Heads of State and Government** of the Member States, its **President** (a new figure in the Union's institutional architecture) and the **President of the Commission**. Under the terms of the Constitution, the new **Minister for Foreign Affairs** of the Union will also take part in the work of the European Council.

A new figure in the Union's institutional landscape: the President of the European Council

Currently, like all the bodies of the Council, the European Council is chaired by the Member State holding the six-month Presidency of the Union, according to a pre-established rota. The Constitution modifies this system by creating a **permanent** function of President of the European Council elected by the European Council for a period of **two-and-a-half years**, renewable once.

The role of this President will be to chair and push forward the work of the European Council. He or she will also serve as a high-level representative of the Union in the area of the common foreign and security policy.

4.1.3 The Council of Ministers

Role of the Council of Ministers

The Council is the Union institution in which the **Governments** of the **Member States** are represented. The Council, with the European Parliament, acts in a legislative and budgetary capacity. It is also the lead institution for decision-making on the common foreign and security policy and on the coordination of economic policies.

Composition of the Council of Ministers

The Council of Ministers is made up of **one representative appointed by each Member State** at ministerial level. It meets in different configurations. Thus, for example, the ministers for agriculture meet in a specific configuration of the Council when it has to take decisions on the common agricultural policy.

At present, all the bodies of the Council are chaired for six months by a single Member State in turn. The Constitution does not make any fundamental changes to this system. However, it has been agreed that the Presidency should be rotated within groups of three countries established for a period of 18 months. This system could change in the future because the European Council will be able to amend it by qualified majority. The "General Affairs" Council will, however, be chaired by the Foreign Affairs Minister. The rules for applying this rota system between the Member States will be established by the European Council, taking due account of the overall geographical balance in Europe, among other things.

Presidency of the Council of Ministers

4.1.4 The European Commission

The Commission was created as an independent body to **represent** the **European interest common** to all the Member States of the Union. It is the driving force of the legislative process, **proposing the "laws"** on which the European Parliament and the Council then have to take a decision.

The Commission's role

The Commission ensures the **planning** and **implementation of the common policies** (e.g. the common agricultural policy), administers the **budget** and **manages** the Community **programmes**. For the day-to-day running of Community policies and programmes, the Commission relies heavily on the national administrations.

Externally, the **Commission represents the Union** and conducts international negotiations (e.g. in the World Trade Organisation). Under the Constitution, the Union's external representation in the area of foreign and security policy will be ensured by the Minister for Foreign Affairs.

Lastly, the Commission **sees to it that the provisions of the Treaty** and decisions taken by the Community institutions, e.g. in the competition sphere, **are correctly applied**.

The Commission is collectively **accountable** to the European Parliament, which may adopt a motion of censure in its regard, whereby the entire Commission must resign as a body.

The Commission is accountable to the European Parliament

The Commission takes its decisions by simple majority.

Composition of the Commission: one commissioner per Member State until 2014, then the Commission members will be limited to two thirds of the number of Member States

Since its inception, the Commission has always **consisted** of two nationals of the most heavily-populated Member States and one national of each of the others. The Treaty of Nice limits the composition of the Commission to one commissioner for each Member State. This is therefore how the Commission to be designated on 1 November 2004 will be composed. The Constitution stipulates that, as of 2014, the Commission will be reduced to the number of members which corresponds to two thirds of the number of Member States. The commissioners will then be chosen according to a system of rotation under which all the Member States will be treated on an equal footing.

Designation of the President of the Commission and the commissioners

The Convention has brought no fundamental changes to the way the **President** of the Commission is appointed but the Constitution indicates clearly that, when proposing to the European Parliament a candidate for the Commission Presidency, the European Council must take account of the results of the European elections.

The Council, in agreement with the Commission President-elect, then adopts the list of future commissioners on the basis of suggestions made by the Member States.

As is already the case, the President and the commissioners, appointed for a five-year term, will be collectively put to a **vote of approval** by the European Parliament.

4.1.5 The Minister for Foreign Affairs

An innovation: the Minister for Foreign Affairs: the Union's voice in the international arena

The creation of the post of Minister for Foreign Affairs is one of the main **innovations** introduced by the Constitution. This function will bring more **consistency** to the Union's external action both at the political and at the economic level. Other countries will **identify the Union's voice more easily**.

This Minister will, to coin a phrase, "wear **two hats**" by performing the tasks currently delegated to two people: the Secretary-General of the Council, High Representative for the common foreign and security policy and the commissioner responsible for external relations. The Foreign Affairs Minister will thus be both the Council's representative for the common foreign and security policy and the member of the Commission responsible for external relations. (He or she will also be one of the Commission's Vice-Presidents.) He or she will chair the Council of Foreign Affairs Ministers and will see to it that the Union's external action is consistent.

Designation of the Minister for Foreign Affairs

The Foreign Affairs Minister will be appointed by qualified majority by the **European Council**, subject to the agreement of the President of the **Commission**.

4.1.6 The Court of Justice of the European Union

The Constitution stipulates that the Court of Justice of the European Union comprises the Court of Justice, the High Court (now called the Court of First Instance) and specialised courts. The Court of Justice and the Court of First Instance are composed of at least one judge per Member State.

Composition of the Court of Justice

The Court of Justice is responsible for **enforcing Community law**. It has jurisdiction in disputes between Member States, between the Union and its Member States, between institutions and between private individuals and the Union. It can also answer questions about the interpretation of Community law raised by national courts in the course of a dispute being heard in such courts. This power to issue preliminary rulings is essential to ensure a uniform interpretation of Community law throughout the Union.

Role of the Court of Justice

The Constitution allows members of the public and businesses to bring an action more easily against the Union's regulatory acts, even if they do not affect them individually (as laid down in the present Treaties).

4.1.7 The European Central Bank (ECB)

The establishment of monetary union and the creation of a single currency, the euro, led to the setting up of the European Central Bank (ECB). Since 1 January 1999, its task has been to conduct European monetary policy as defined by the European System of Central Banks (ESCB). In concrete terms, the ECB's decision-making bodies (the governing council and the executive board) direct the European System of Central Banks in order to manage monetary growth, carry out exchange operations, hold and manage the official exchange reserves of the Member States and ensure the smooth running of payments systems. The primary aim of the ECB is to maintain price stability.

The European Central Bank conducts European monetary policy

4.1.8 The Court of Auditors

The Court of Auditors **monitors** the European Union's accounts, examining the legality and regularity of revenue and expenditure in the Union's **budget** and ensuring sound financial management. It is composed of one national from each Member State.

The Court of Auditors monitors revenue and expenditure

4.1.9 The Committee of the Regions

The Committee of the Regions: an advisory body

The Committee of the Regions comprises representatives of **local and regional authorities**. It is **consulted** by Parliament, the Council and the Commission in areas affecting regional and local interests, including education, public health, and economic and social cohesion.

Composition of the Committee of the Regions

The number of members of the Committee of the Regions is established at a maximum of 350. They are appointed for a five-year period by the Council.

4.1.10 The European Economic and Social Committee [1]

The European Economic and Social Committee: an advisory body

The European Economic and Social Committee (EESC), made up **of representatives of the economic and social sectors and of civil society**, gives **advisory opinions** to the institutions, particularly in the context of the legislative procedure. The EESC is consulted by the European Parliament, the Council or the Commission, ahead of the adoption of many acts concerning the internal market, education, consumer protection, the environment, regional development and the social sphere.

Composition of the European Economic and Social Committee

The number of members of the Economic and Social Committee has been established at a maximum of 350. These members are appointed by the Council for a period of five years.

[1] Economic and Social Committee according to the terminology used in the Constitutional Treaty.

5. The Union's means of action

5.1 Simplification of instruments

Simplification of the instruments for action at the Union's disposal took up a specific chapter of the Laeken Declaration, which established the Convention's mandate. The work of the Convention has made it possible to **simplify** the existing system.

Simplifying the instruments whereby the Union exercises its powers

The typology of acts is limited to **six instruments** (law, framework law, regulation, decision, recommendation and opinion). In a famous speech prior to the Laeken European Council, the Belgian Prime Minister had noted the existence of 36 different types of act!

Six legal instruments

The hierarchy between the legislative level and the level for implementing laws is established, as in all national legal systems.

Legislative level and level of implementation

The **law** will determine the essential elements of a given area, while the definition of more technical aspects may be delegated to the Commission under the supervision of two co-legislators. This will lighten the workload of the latter, who can then focus on the more important aspects of the life of the people of Europe.

Under the terms of the Constitution, the Commission will be responsible for adopting delegated regulations which supplement and/or amend certain non-essential elements of the law, subject to the control of the co-legislators. Amendments to non-essential elements of the law

Amendments to non-essential elements of the law

5.2 Legislative procedure

The **legislative procedure** currently known as the codecision procedure gives the **European Parliament** power as **co-legislator** on an equal footing with the **Council**. Under the terms of this procedure, a text proposed by the Commission, once the interested parties have been consulted, is adopted both by the European Parliament and by the Council.

Parliament and the Council co-legislate

The generalisation of the codecision procedure which the Constitution establishes as an ordinary legislative procedure conveys the best image of the dual legitimacy of the States (Council) and peoples (European Parliament), which is the hallmark of the Union. However, in certain cases there will be special laws, adopted by the Council alone or, more rarely, by the European Parliament alone. The Constitution stipulates that the Council takes decisions by majority voting except when the Constitution makes provision for another procedure, such as unanimous voting.

Voting within the Council

Definition of qualified majority

The "qualified majority" is at present calculated using a weighting system which takes account, to some extent, of the population of individual Member States. The Constitution introduces, from 2009, a **new definition of qualified majority** in the Council: this is a **double majority** of Member States and peoples, who represent the dual legitimacy of the Union. A double majority is achieved when a decision is taken by 55% of the Member States representing at least 65% of the Union's population.

Scope of the qualified majority

The extension of **qualified majority voting** in the Council, envisaged by the Constitution for some twenty provisions for which unanimity is currently required, will make it easier to take decisions. Unanimous voting and hence the possibility for a single Member State to prevent a decision from being taken has been maintained, for instance, for taxation-related measures stemming from the internal market or minimum requirements with regard to social security. However, a "bridging" provision in the Constitution allows a future change to qualified majority voting on the basis of a unanimous decision of the European Council.

Specific decisions relating to the CFSP

Specific decision-making arrangements are envisaged with regard to the common foreign and security policy, including the European security and defence policy.

Forging ahead in enhanced cooperation without all parties being involved

In order to foster closer cooperation between those countries of the Union wishing, in a given context corresponding to the objectives of the Union but which is not part of its exclusive competence, to go beyond the level of integration envisaged in the Treaties, the Amsterdam Treaty introduced the concept of "enhanced cooperation". The aim of this type of cooperation is to enable a limited number of Member States, capable and eager to do so, to move ahead with European integration, in full respect of the Union's institutional framework.

This enhanced cooperation can be used only as a last resort (when the objectives of such cooperation cannot be attained by the Union as a whole); it requires a minimum of Member States (the Constitution establishes this number at one third of the Member States) and all the Member States must be free to join in at a later stage. Acts adopted through enhanced cooperation are binding only on the Member States involved.

5.3 The Union's finances

The Community **budget** follows traditional budgetary patterns and is therefore founded on certain principles: unity (overall expenditure and revenue in a single document), annuality (budgetary operations are linked to a financial year) and balance (expenditure must not exceed revenue).

The Constitution stipulates that a European law introduced by the Council, acting by unanimous vote, will lay down the **"multiannual financial framework"** and annual ceilings for the Union's expenditure. The budget must comply with this multiannual financial framework.

The budget is funded by the Union's **own resources** which are primarily made up of a proportion of the VAT levied by the Member States and a certain percentage of the GNP of the Member States. The limits and categories of these resources are established by the Council and must also be ratified by all the Member States.

The Commission has the task of presenting the draft annual budget for the Union. The Constitution envisages the adoption of the budget by the **European Parliament** and the **Council**, which together **form the budgetary authority**, using a much simpler procedure than that currently applied.

The **Commission** implements the budget under the supervision of the European Parliament and the Court of Auditors. In practice, a very high proportion of the budget is implemented on a daily basis by the Member States, particularly as regards those sections which relate to agriculture.

Side notes:
- The Union's budget
- The multi-annual financial framework
- Own resources
- Budgetary procedure
- Implementation of the budget

6. The Union's external action

All the Union's external action presented under a single title: better readability and greater consistency

The provisions relating to the Union's external action have all been **grouped** under a single title in the Constitution, whereas they featured in the previous Treaties in a number of different places. This has improved the **readability** of the text. This grouping also permits **greater consistency of Union action** in relation to third countries, in as much as all actions, be they economic, humanitarian or political, have common objectives.

Maintenance of unanimity

With regard to foreign policy, the Council will continue to decide **unanimously** in most cases. The Constitution has not shown the progress hoped for by some on this point. In a Union of 25 or 30 States, unanimity, i.e. the right of veto for every Member State, will not make decision-making any easier!
Maintenance of unanimity

An innovation: the creation of the post of Minister for Foreign Affairs of the Union

The most interesting innovation is the creation of the post of **Minister for Foreign Affairs**. He/she will be **Vice-President of the Commission** but will work directly with the **Member States** on foreign policy issues. The introduction of this new function should foster mutual trust and the European instinct of the Member States. The person concerned will be in charge of a European external action service and of a diplomatic service, which will be composed of officials from the Council, the Commission and the national diplomatic services and will have delegations in almost every country of the world. The Foreign Affairs Minister will ensure that the Union is more effective and has a stronger voice on the international stage. He/she can for instance speak on behalf of the Union in the United Nations Security Council.

A European defence policy which respects the political commitments of the Member States

The Union's **defence policy** is slowly taking shape, in full respect of the different cultures and political commitments of the Member States (there is no question of ending the neutrality of certain Member States or of vying with NATO).

Creation of an Armaments Agency

An **Armaments Agency** will be set up so that the taxpayers' money is better used, avoiding, for instance, duplication in the military programmes of the different Member States.

Solidarity between the Member States, e.g. in the event of a terrorist attack

By joining the Union, the Member States are agreed on mutual solidarity. This **solidarity** is not simply economic: in the event of a **terrorist** attack or natural **disaster**, the Constitution henceforth provides for action by the Union. Moreover, if one Member State is the victim of armed aggression on its territory, the other Member States must give it aid and assistance.

Possibility of permanent structured defence cooperation between certain Member States

The Constitution also enables Member States with the necessary military capabilities and which have made more binding commitments to establish a permanent cooperation structure between themselves within the Union.

With regard to **external trade**, it is the **Commission** which **negotiates, on behalf of the Union as a whole, with non-member countries**, particularly the World Trade Organisation, to defend European interests with regard to trading in goods and services, intellectual property and investment.

External trade: the Commission negotiates with non-member countries

In this area, the Constitution enhances the role of the **European Parliament**, which is placed virtually on an equal footing with the Council, whereas hitherto the Treaty gave it no role either in monitoring or decision-making. The **Council's** decision-making rules are also made clearer so as to allow the Union to continue to be an indispensable player in the regulation of the world economy.

More power for the European Parliament, clearer decision-making rules within the Council

The principle aim of the **Union's development policy** is the eradication of poverty. The Union and its Member States account for over 50% of public aid in the world; in the interests of greater effectiveness, proper coordination of their action in pursuit of this aim is essential.

A development policy focusing on the eradication of poverty

One Constitutional provision focuses on the **Union's humanitarian aid policy** (managed by ECHO) in order to show its specific nature (it complies with international humanitarian law and is not a means of political pressure).

Humanitarian aid policy

The Constitution specifies how and when the Union can negotiate **international agreements**, and it sets out clearly the procedure to be followed: the Commission (or the Foreign Affairs Minister) negotiates, and the Council and the European Parliament decide jointly whether they accept the outcome.

Negotiation of international agreements

7. An area of freedom, security and justice

Appropriate means to act together against terrorism and crime

The concept of an area of freedom, security and justice already features in the current Treaties. However, the Constitution gives the Union **appropriate** means of reaching solutions consonant with the scale of the challenge facing the Union (how to ensure the free movement of people, how to fight against terrorism and serious crime, how to manage migratory flows). The Constitution also makes the applicable procedures **more effective**, **more democratic and more transparent**.

Absence of internal border controls. Control of the Union's external borders

As already provided for in the current Treaties, the Constitution establishes, for the Member States which form part of the **"Schengen area"**, **the absence of controls at the Union's internal borders**, and will establish rules for the checks applicable to people crossing its **external borders**. Furthermore, the Union may manage its borders in an integrated way, which means, for instance, setting up a unit which can assist and support national border guards in their difficult tasks of controlling and monitoring borders.

Common policy on asylum

The Union must have a **genuine common policy on asylum**, fully respecting the Geneva Convention on refugees and ensuring that any person needing international protection is effectively afforded such protection. Unlike the current Treaties, which provide simply for the establishment of minimum rules, the Constitution provides for the establishment of a **common European asylum system** which includes, inter alia, a **uniform status** for refugees and **common procedures**.

Common immigration policy

The Union will also introduce a **common policy on immigration**. The Constitution sets out the guiding principles of this common policy, which the existing Treaties did not do. The point is to manage flows effectively, ensure fair treatment for immigrants who are legally resident, and prevent and counter illegal immigration and people trafficking. The Council and the European Parliament will take steps to this effect, for instance with regard to the conditions applicable to immigration into the Member States or with regard to immigrants' rights. The Union may also adopt measures to support the Member States' efforts to integrate the nationals of third countries.

A solidary Union and democratic procedures

These policies will all be conducted in full respect of the **principle of solidarity**, including financial solidarity, which is enshrined in the Constitution. Democratic legitimacy will be considerably strengthened. Indeed, under the current Treaties, the European Parliament is merely consulted whereas in the Constitution all these measures are adopted by the European Parliament and the Council. Another major change concerns the Court of Justice, which will exercise its jurisdictional control on all acts adopted; lastly, the Commission will be the only source of legislative initiative and will also continue its role as guardian of the Treaties.

As is already the case, the Union will continue to act in the area of **judicial cooperation in civil matters**, provided the matters in question are of cross-border relevance. Unlike the existing Treaties, the Constitution gives the Council and the European Parliament the power to adopt laws or framework laws to ensure a high level of access to justice.

Judicial cooperation in civil matters

Under the terms of the current Treaties, the Union could already act in the area of **police and judicial cooperation on criminal matters**. However, as in the case of the common foreign and security policy, this was handled in a separate part of the Treaty on European Union, known as the third pillar and subject to the intergovernmental decision-making method. The Constitution innovates in this area by doing away with the third pillar, grouping within a single structure all the Union's policies, and introducing procedures which are more democratic, **more effective and more transparent**. One special feature: a group of Member States (a quarter) can submit an initiative in the same way as the Commission. The right of veto is to a very large extent dropped in favour of the qualified majority rule; the Parliament co-legislates with the Council and the rules adopted must be submitted to the scrutiny of the Court of Justice.

Police and judicial cooperation on criminal matters

The European Parliament and the Council can thus establish common definitions and **penalties** in respect of a series of **serious and cross-border offences** which are listed in the Constitution. These are very serious crimes, such as terrorism, drug trafficking, people trafficking, racism and xenophobia, sexual exploitation of children and environmental crime.

Common penalties against cross-border offences

The Constitution will also enable the Union to adopt framework laws on criminal procedure, with regard to the rights of victims and personal rights in criminal procedure. The mechanisms for judicial cooperation between Member States which already exist, e.g. Eurojust, will be strengthened and the Council may at some time in the future decide to introduce a **European prosecutor's department** to track down and prosecute the perpetrators of and accomplices in serious cross-border crimes. This decision will be taken unanimously by the Member States.

Possibility of creating a European prosecutor's department to prosecute those guilty of cross-border crime

In the area of **police cooperation**, the European Police Office, Europol, offers a structure for developing police cooperation between Member States in the prevention and combating of all serious forms of organised international crime. Under the Constitution, Europol will be subject to the scrutiny of the European Parliament and of the national parliaments.

Police cooperation

8. The Union's other policies: what the Constitution contributes

Reform of certain Union policies

The Convention and the Intergovernmental Conference focused particular attention on the **reform of certain policies** (common foreign and security policy; area of freedom, security and justice; economic and monetary union). However, there were no major changes to the Union's other policies. Contrary to some of the previous revisions of the Treaties (Single Act and Maastricht Treaty), the Constitution has not significantly extended the Union's powers.

Consistency of Union action

Special attention was devoted to maintaining **consistency in Union action**, through provisions to ensure that the overall objectives - and more particularly gender equality, the environment, consumers - are taken into account when defining and implementing each specific policy.

New scope for action in certain areas

The Constitution introduces **new legal bases** which will allow the Union to take action if need be in the areas of: public **health**, in response to common concerns affecting the security of the general public (e.g. SARS, bio-terrorism); **energy**, in order to promote access to public service, its continuity, security of supply, the development of renewable sources of energy and energy saving; **civil protection**, to assist Member States to deal with natural or man-made disasters; and **sport**, to develop its educational dimension and coordinate efforts to prevent doping.

9. Entry into force and revision of the Constitution

Entry into force of the Constitution

Entry into force of the Constitution

The constitutional Treaty is based on the assumption that it will be ratified by all the Member States in line with their own constitutional rules (by parliamentary approval and/or by referendum). If, after two years following its signature, only four-fifths of the Member States have ratified it, the European Council will review the situation.

Subsequent revisions of the Constitution

Revision of the Constitution: confirmation of the Convention method

From now on, revisions will normally be prepared by a Convention, unless their scope is limited. The Convention must adopt by consensus a recommendation to the Intergovernmental Conference, which will jointly agree on the amendments to be introduced. These amendments will enter into force only when they have been ratified by all the Member States in accordance with their respective constitutional arrangements.

A more flexible procedure is envisaged for certain amendments such as the extension of the scope of qualified majority voting to certain fields of action. For such amendments, the unanimous agreement of the European Council and the approval of the European Parliament will be sufficient.